Key Acknowledgements

Michael Lim

To Alice, my wife for having the patience and understanding during the early years. To Jing and Ling, my lovely daughters, for being an inspiration in my life and showing me the true joys of Living Kaizen.To my 5S gurus; Mr. Masao Umeda (Toshiba Group), Mr. Norio Suzuki (Consulting Bell Service), Dr. Seiichi Fujita (AOTS) and Mr. Shuichi Yoshida (GTR Consulting), thank you for your wisdom & guidance.

Chee Iihann

To Mum & Dad, for their selfless dedication and Living Kaizen attitude in supporting me through the best and worst of times. Love you both.To Janice, my darling wife. Thank you so much for your unconditional love and support and for proving to me that the dark is just a state of the mind -- and to turn on the light.

Contents

Foreword

We all want happiness, and we are very fortunate to have access to many different ways and means to find that happiness. Indeed finding joy and happiness should become the primary concern for all people, because only by finding their own happiness, will happiness spread.

This book was written to help those who want change, but are unable to do so without some form of system or logical framework to work with. One of the fundamental tenets that support *Living Kaizen* include the now famous *Universal Law of Attraction*. This universal concept of physics has received great attention amongst gurus and men of science. Indeed, it was the manifestation of this powerful and unique Law that this book and the amazing journey could be possible.

Two ingredients were necessary in making this book a reality. The first was the meeting of 2 completely different individuals, united by the compassion and the realization of their life purpose — and from that synergy, a powerful desire was formed to help people find greater clarity and joy in their lives. The second ingredient was a traditional code of conduct — which apart from its practice in certain manufacturing and processing industries, no one bothered about. However, the inherent power of this Japanese discipline formed the basis of which we saw the possibility for innovation and transformation. At that point, we decided that the only way to validate it would be to live it and practise the systematic, yet adaptable techniques we innovated. The rest, as they say is history, and the story of that success formed the basis of *Living Kaizen*'s story.

The sole purpose of this book is to be a compass for people who have a strong desire for change, but are not able to crystallize a workable, practical plan of action. While we would be the first to state that *Living Kaizen* may not be the right cup of tea for everyone, we do believe that *Living Kaizen* does play a valuable role as a powerful tool to solve challenges and issues of contrast in our daily lives. It is a valuable discipline that when habituated, will help you find and sustain that critical vibrational frequency or state of mind that will propel you to achieve your goals and desires.

Living Kaizen fulfills a powerful proactive role in ensuring that the mind and the body are attuned and in constant motion of thoughts and deeds that put a person closer to goals and dreams in a measurable, step by step manner. You could say that *Living Kaizen* forms the missing "actionable" portion of attaining one's dreams and desires. There are many books that do a wonderful job of aligning a person's concepts of being. *Living Kaizen* leverages on the scenario that the person has achieved a level of consciousness and is looking for measurable means to practice habituating and being in the constant state of alignment with what they want.

Is that a tall order? Far from it. This book is proof that *Living Kaizen* works and continues to work. It is with great excitement and hope that anyone looking to make measurable changes in their life will find the stories and wisdom contained in this book a valuable tool that will help them get it and find joy getting it.

"*Every person's life experience is unique and different, hence it is the individuality of wisdom attained that makes being human so special.*" — *Iihann*

Chapter 1 — What the heck is Living Kaizen?

It was a warm April evening when Michael trudged wearily to a meeting point at a prominent shopping complex. He was supposed to meet some guy that would apparently help him structure and plan his Kaizen posters. As he was highly recommended by a friend, Michael decided to meet up with him quickly.

Blinking his eyes blearily at the throngs of shoppers, he caught a glimpse of an overweight bespectacled guy with a smiling expression on his face.

"That must be the guy. I hope this meeting will be fruitful," thought Michael.

Michael came from a manufacturing and training background. With over 24 years under his belt, he was a seasoned, if not tired practitioner of many venerable production disciplines and processes. However, his forte came from training and teaching the principles of Kaizen — a highly disciplined manufacturing and production housekeeping system created in Japan in the aftermath of the Second World War. It was this system that forged Japan's industrial strength and allowed the country to bounce back to the world economy in 30 years.

Bred tough and bitter from the slums of Kuala Lumpur, Michael had fought tooth and nail for every thing he had in life —

1

from his ascension through the rank and file to his independence as an entrepreneur. Despite his fighting spirit, his passion for helping others often came under tremendous pressures — from his contemporaries who made a lot of money milking the economy to members of his extended family who couldn't understand why he chose his path. And the pressures were beginning to exact a toll on him and his family.

"Hi Michael, How are you? My name's Ian!" The spirited greeting jolted Michael out of his reverie as he shook hands with Ian.

"At least the description is apt," thought Michael remembering his friend's amusing description of Ian resembling a boisterous laughing God of Prosperity from Chinese mythology. As they found themselves seats in a nearby Japanese restaurant, Michael couldn't help but notice the relaxed manner in which Ian carried himself. After ordering their food, Michael decided to get on to it and starting talking about himself.

During the meeting that followed, Michael spoke about the task at hand, which was essentially some copywriting work he needed for Kaizen posters he was selling. Those posters were important to him, for they helped him pay the bills — and there were an awful lot of bills.

As Michael spoke, he noted that Ian's jovial manner gradually became more serious and thoughtful. Ian didn't speak much, except to ask for clarification on certain aspects of Michael's career, about *Kaizen* and the Japanese housekeeping system. At some point, Michael fell silent, having exhausted his vocal cords answering Ian's queries and looked expectantly at the equally silent Ian.

After taking a deep breath, Ian spoke. "Michael, do you know what you have here?" His keen eyes bored into Michael's.

What is he talking about? Hasn't he been listening to what I have been saying for the past hour? Michael groaned inwardly.

"Do you realize that this is more than just a discipline for the manufacturing industry? It is a powerful basis for a living discipline that can appeal to those who are ready to move forward in life." Ian spoke with a sudden passion that surprised Michael.

"Let me clarify this." Ian explained. "It's really easy for me to just help you with whatever you wanted to do with your posters. I could just charge you a fee and walk away from this."

"But my gut feeling tells me that there's far greater potential for you to help other people with this," Ian declared.

"Well, it's a housekeeping system, so I guess people who want to be tidy and neat could benefit," Michael replied, thoughtfully rubbing his chin.

"Michael, that's not really going to help people you know," sighed Ian.

"What I am saying is that you should look beyond what it is, think out of the box and transform it into a tool that will truly benefit humanity," continued Ian in earnest.

Help people? Michael knew he was already helping people. If only those hard-headed managers would listen then.

"Michael, I sense great unhappiness in you," Ian said. "No, I am not a psychic — but it doesn't take a psychic to tell me that you think you are at the bottom of a deep dark hole, and it's so hard trying to dig yourself out."

This guy is perceptive, Michael thought. Maybe Ian would give me a discount on his services.

"Michael, listen to me. Do you truly want change in your life? Or do you just want to sell posters for the rest of your life?" Ian's statement jolted Michael out of his thoughts.

"Of course I want change. I used to drive a nice SUV, go for seafood dinners every week, even buy my daughters nice things," Michael responded bitterly. "I can barely make ends meet, what with my girls in school and all."

Ian leaned closer, the lights from the restaurant momentarily reflecting off his spectacles.

"Then I have a proposition for you. It's no coincidence that we met up. I sense deep pain, resentment and anger within you. But I also sense that you believe in helping people better themselves, am I correct?" Ian probed.

"Yes — and maybe that's my karma," responded Michael, evoking his oft-used excuse.

"But you aren't giving yourself the chance to change for the better. I am not one to knock religion, but blaming it on karma and such isn't going to help you turn your life around." Ian's voice took on a slightly harder edge. "So let me ask you one more time. Do you want change?"

"Yes — yes, I do want change," admitted Michael. "Can you help me change, since you seem to know what you are talking about?"

Ian beamed, his cherubic face lighting up again. "Yes I can — but you must make a commitment to stick with the program — or else it would be both a waste of my time and yours."

"I promise, I will commit." said Michael "But while you are helping me with whatever you say you are going to help me — what about my posters?"

"That is precisely what you will discover. Kaizen isn't merely a philosophy and a set of housekeeping systems — well it won't be once we're done with it," Ian said with a sly wink. "But what you will discover in the coming weeks and months, is that Kaizen is going to become something far, far more amazing than you have ever imagined."

"When do I meet you next?" Michael asked.

"Good question. Let's meet up every Wednesday night at my place. You got e-mail? I will e-mail my address details to you," Ian answered.

"Ok. I will bring my Kaizen posters over so you can take a look at them." Michael said.

"Uh — Michael — those posters are going to be the last thing on your mind when we are done." said Ian. "By the way, it's going to be *Living Kaizen* now, because where we will be going with this, it's going to come alive in ways you never thought possible!"

Michael was mildly disturbed by Ian's gleeful expression, but kept his thoughts to himself. After all, he reasoned, Ian didn't seem to be the type to trap him with some get-rich-quick scheme. As Michael left the restaurant, he hoped that whatever ideas Ian had for his Kaizen — no, *Living Kaizen* process, it would help him land a few more sales for his posters.

 Points to ponder

What is Living Kaizen? At its essence, Living Kaizen is a formula that is highly adaptable to initiate change. Many systems known to Man are usually fixed and cannot be made to adapt easily. However, because every person's contrasting experience is different and unique; Living Kaizen adapts to that individual's experience, and when practiced correctly will yield individually powerful results.

Living Kaizen owes its origins to Kaizen, a unique concept involving simple disciplines of continuous improvement and is credited to have been created in Japan during the post-war years. Its essence and wisdom is prevalent in its practice in various forms amongst the world's most successful conglomerates. The Kaizen concept has since been incorporated into many other proprietary processes, but its essence, which focuses on the uniquely human concept of "taking responsibility", is pervasive, even in the most high-tech arenas other than production. Powerful Japanese companies have Kaizen disciplines imbued into the very fabric of their systems from human resource to planning.

What is apparent however is that Living Kaizen has taken this discipline a step further, by understanding that for as long as taking responsibility is a unique human trait, an adaptive problem-solving discipline can be manifested in any human experience regardless of its unique qualities. This concept is powerful just in its understanding and it is imperative that practitioners of Living Kaizen believe in fundamental principles i.e. the universal Law of Attraction. It is also key that without human will and focus, Living Kaizen will not be able to fulfill its purpose. For it is human will and focus that life pursues its purpose. Without a goal or a dream or even a wish, there is <u>not enough responsibility</u> in the individual to be in a state of mind of <u>wanting to achieve.</u> This is the paradox of human will and life purpose. By understanding that, anyone who wants to achieve anything can do so. Living Kaizen takes on a whole new level as its logical, step-by-step process allows a person to focus on measurable results that ultimately deliver the goal or that dream.

Chapter 2 — Sorting out your life

"......and so I was hoping that with all my problems maybe there's a way I can use your help to solve them..." Michael finished and lapsed into silence.

Michael was sitting in Ian's cozy living room area. The week before had passed very quickly, and Michael was secretly hoping that Ian wasn't going to snare him with a hare-brained scheme or business. Ian's modest terraced home seemed a harmless example of modern suburbia.

Ian blinked.

And blinked again.

He took a deep breath, took off his spectacles and said quietly. "Thank you for sharing your thoughts with me." His demeanor suddenly took on a more serious look. "But I would like us to look into what you have been telling me for the last twenty minutes..."

"Did you realize the tone and manner in which you were speaking to me?"

Michael was puzzled, and shook his head, wondering if he did missed out any important pieces of information that prompted this question.

Unperturbed, Ian continued. "Let me answer that question for you. The last twenty minutes of your conversation was completely in the negative. While I believe that everything that was said was spoken from experience — it is amazing that there is so much unhappiness contained in those memories. That will be the first challenge that we need to work out together."

"We need to understand first where I am coming from before we begin to *Sort* out this issue. You see, all our actions or results of our thoughts are but an endless cycle brought about by our beliefs, yes?"

To illustrate his point, Ian pulled out a clean sheet of paper and commenced drawing...

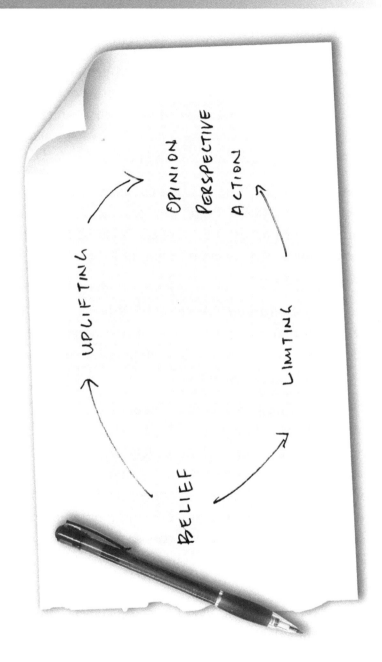

"This diagram is pretty universal and most people would recognize this principle. However, our challenge is to go back to the root of everything, and the root of all action is in the belief system. This belief system may get its power from either the past, present or the future — it does not matter. What matters is that we need to understand the belief — and *Sort* out what is necessary in order to begin the process of healing or resolution."

Something struck Michael at this stage, and he asked. "In Kaizen, whenever one is faced with a situation of disorder, the first principle that needs to be applied would be to identify what are the key areas that are contributing to the problem. Does that then apply in my case?"

Ian's eyes lighted up. "Absolutely! When you first put your beliefs under a microscope, you must first understand the root cause of these beliefs. It's a key element in first *Sorting* out your life."

"All beliefs are a product of our unconscious mind. However, while we'd like to think that most of our actions are controlled by our conscious mind, unfortunately they aren't. Whatever we experience, be it past, present or future, these experiences generate reactions within us. Our unconscious mind then makes silent agreements which form the basis of a belief system. However, depending on the experience, our unconscious mind cannot differentiate between creating an uplifting belief or limiting belief."

"But that's why *Sorting* out your core beliefs is critical moving towards crafting a positive affirmation or releasing negative ones."

12

Ian's eyes narrowed. "But the challenge isn't just merely identifying where those beliefs come from. It's much more than that."

"There are 3 word categories I would like to acquaint you with regards to work out this area. Many people don't realize it but a lot of times their words often fall into these 3 categories. They are *justification, laying blame* and *taking responsibility.*"

Michael looked at Ian quizzically as he continued. "Justifying your actions or laying blame on situations and people are the worse things you can do when you *Sort* out the beliefs in your mind. This is because your conscious mind is playing a big part in trying to protect you from seeing the truth of events as they are. The enemy of justification and laying blame is taking responsibility. By taking responsibility of the issues that created the belief, you are then able to wholeheartedly release them or strengthen them to your benefit."

"Remember the last time we met? I broached the idea of you sharing your learning experience by launching your book?"

Michael groaned when he remembered that conversation and said. "Yes, it was a book on processes and principles but at this juncture, I do not have the resources. Selling the Kaizen posters is where I barely make my living. Add on to that....."

Ian rolled his eyes and started waving his hands. "Wait, just wait. Did you realize what you just did? You blamed your current lack of resources for not giving you the opportunity to complete and publish your book. You also justified being unable to take the time out to finish and work towards producing the book. That is your conscious mind making excuses to cover up your belief systems. If you want change, you must take responsibility for your actions. Otherwise, you will never be able to break the cycle of negativity and failure."

Silence reigned as Michael digested this. "Where do I start?"

"At the very beginning of course! Ha! Ha! Pardon the pun." Ian laughed. "First of all you need to get a grip on your entire belief system. You need to do a *Sorting Board* that captures all major memories and beliefs that are clogging your mind at the moment. This *Sorting Board* will allow you to categorize into manageable chunks of beliefs. You will be surprised as to how many of your beliefs are centered on only a few experiences. Once you have completed your *Sorting Board*, you will need to focus on the belief chunks and once you trace these back to the fundamental experiences, you need to take responsibility for them."

"Whoa, how do I do that?" asked Michael. Ian grinned."Ok, let's take an example of you having issues in communicating with your children that you have highlighted on your *Sorting Board*. In our discussion we managed to trace it back to your childhood experience. Is that not so?" asked Ian.

"Yes, but then how -?"

"When we delved into it a bit further we realized that you had a broken childhood where your father left you at an early age. That made a distinctive impact on your unconscious mind — however it left you without a reference point on how to be a father. Take the first step by *acknowledging* and *taking responsibility* for feeling the pain and unhappiness then. Once you have firmly faced this, you can then use special affirmations to release these thoughts and replace them with positive ones. For example, you can choose to say, "I take responsibility for feeling let down and disappointed that my father left me to fend for myself. I release the fear and pain I felt during that time. I am now a father of my children. Those feelings do not serve me. I release them now. So be it."

Highly skeptical, Michael asked. "Is that it? Are you sure saying stuff like that will work?"

His face crinkling in amusement, Ian replied. "Don't take my word for it. Do it and let me know."

 Points to ponder

That meeting had the beginnings of a profound effect on Michael. Before, he was loaded down only with bad memories of his past failures in his relationships and business, further strengthened by his many negative unconscious thoughts and beliefs.

In that aspect, many of you who are reading this may find that Michael's experiences mirror your own. The point being made is — so what?

It is said that almost 90% of most people's childhood experiences are not considered normal. Hence, bad experiences such as abuse, broken homes etc. are merely the conditions in which our earliest beliefs were programmed. The beauty of Living Kaizen is that as its first principle, we must face the root of all that we are. Through a simple exercise of creating a Sorting Board, which is in effect, a board containing either pictures or words that depict what your beliefs and thoughts are — you begin a healing process of identifying the basis of how you behave and do everyday.

It's critical at this stage that those who attempt the Sorting Board do so over a period of time as some memories that trigger beliefs may be too traumatic or disturbing. This portion becomes the most challenging for many as they have to get past the justification and blame-laying tricks played by their conscious mind. When the core emotions or topics are revealed, the next process in Sorting would be to acknowledge those thoughts and release them.

MICHAEL'S SORTING BOARD

CREATIVE

PERSEVERENCE (PATIENCE)

PASSIONATE ABOUT HELPING PEOPLE

CAREFUL / METICULOUS

CARE FOR THE FAMILY

NOT ANALYTICAL

STUBBORN

STRONGWILLED

CONSERVATIVE

LECTURER MINDED

EMOTIONALLY UNSTABLE

NOT CLOSE TO FAMILY

JUSTIFYING WITH EXCUSES

BLAME SITUATION ON OTHERS

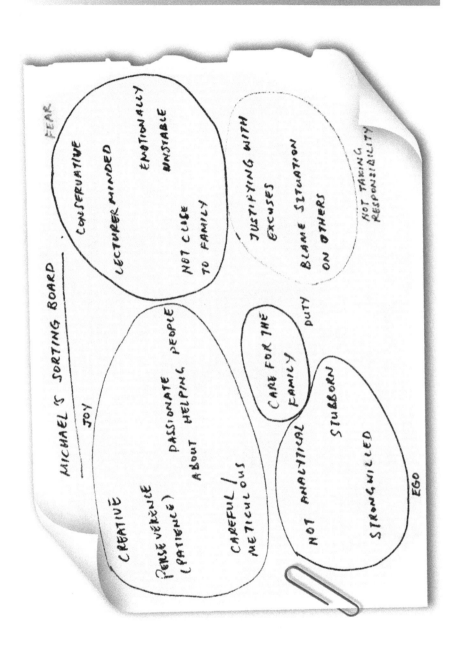

MICHAEL'S SORTING BOARD

JOY

FEAR

CONSERVATIVE
LECTURER MINDED
EMOTIONALLY UNSTABLE
NOT CLOSE TO FAMILY

JUSTIFYING WITH EXCUSES
BLAME SITUATION ON OTHERS
NOT TAKING RESPONSIBILITY

CREATIVE
PERSEVERENCE (PATIENCE)
PASSIONATE ABOUT HELPING PEOPLE
CAREFUL / METICULOUS

CARE FOR THE FAMILY
DUTY

NOT ANALYTICAL
STUBBORN
STRONGWILLED

EGO

18

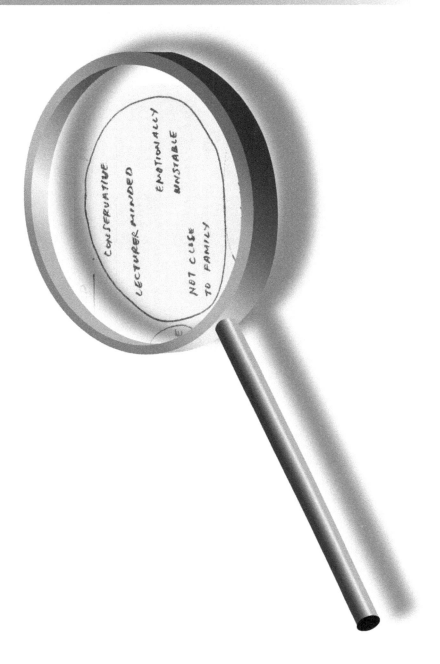

LIMITING BELIEFS

STEP ONE
- ACKNOWLEDGEMENT
  STATEMENT

I ACKNOWLEDGE
THE FEAR TO CHANGE
AND ACCEPT CHANGE,
THE FEAR THAT MY
OPINIONS WILL NOT BE
ACCEPTED NOR RESPECTED

THE FEAR THAT I AM NOT
A GOOD FATHER

THE FEAR THAT THINGS
ARE NOT DONE RIGHT WILL
REFLECT POORLY ON ME
WHICH MAKES ME LOOK
STUPID

FEAR

EGO

NOT TAKING
RESPONSIBILITY

LIMITING BELIEFS

STEP TWO – RELEASING STATEMENT

I RELEASE TO FEEL THE FEAR
TO CHANGE AND ACCEPT CHANGE.
TO FEAR THAT MY OPINIONS
WILL NOT BE ACCEPTED NOR
RESPECTED, TO FEAR THAT I
AM NOT A GOOD FATHER,
TO FEAR THAT THINGS NOT
DONE RIGHT WILL REFLECT
POORLY ON ME MAKING ME
LOOK STUPID.

THESE FEARS DO NOT SERVE ME.

I RELEASE THESE FEARS AND TO
FEEL THESE FEARS ANYMORE.

I RELEASE THEM NOW!

SO BE IT!

FEAR

EGO

NOT TAKING RESPONSIBILITY

There were many questions in Michael's mind when he next met up with Ian. Bringing his *Sorting Board* with him, Michael framed his questions carefully as Ian settled himself down.

"Ian, I discovered quite a few unpleasant beliefs that I was not fully aware of. I also realized that my childhood played a far bigger role in creating my beliefs than I anticipated. But the question is, how do I move forward despite acknowledging these beliefs or even trying to release these negative thoughts — how do I move forward to achieve my goals and dreams?"

"You are absolutely spot on with your observations," Ian smiled. "Belief systems can be identified but more importantly you need to either replace them with positive ones or re-program them."

Ian leaned back. "There are many tools and systems out there that teach you how to re-program beliefs and unconscious agreements. And while each tool has its purpose, in your case your challenge requires a far more in-depth and personalized experience to fix these beliefs."

"For starters, here's an exercise I would like to do now that requires you to have fun!" Ian's eyes twinkled in amusement at Michael's surprise. "Not everything needs to be that serious. Imagine for example that you were given an unlimited bank account and that you can write yourself cheques that increase by $10,000 each month…"

"That would be very nice indeed," quipped Michael.

"Ha! Well now's your chance to see how you are going to spend your first $10K. The condition is that you must fully utilize the money in your cheque. No "saving for a rainy day" thinking here. Here you go — $10K. What are you going to spend it on? Let your imagination soar and write it down!" encouraged Ian, while handling Michael a couple of sheets of paper and a pen.

"Hmmmm….let's see….," Michael started to scribble.

An hour and approximately $300K later, Michael conceded defeat. "I seem to have run out of things to spend."

Ian chortled and said, "Well, you certainly had quite a fair bit of ideas on how to spend your money!"

"Well it's easy when I don't have to worry about my kids or survival or putting food on the table, you know," Michael mused. "What I am curious about is the intent of this exercise — however enjoyable it was — and how it plays a role in changing my beliefs or getting me closer to my dreams."

"The purpose of this exercise is not to find your wish-list based on how much you earn. The purpose is to determine what your priorities are and draw the link between your inner self and the results of your *Sorting Board*. This exercise allows cross-checking and validation to ensure your conscious mind isn't playing tricks on you," Ian explained, taking Michael's sheet of paper and poring through his wish-list.

"Hmmmm...very interesting..." Ian said thoughtfully.

"It would seem that from this exercise, you want quite a fair bit of things for yourself — not a crime in itself for it is only natural that we would want nice things for ourselves. However, this draws a direct link between your key fear you discovered which was *Fear of Self-Ego* and the items you would want to buy for yourself."

"Really? How can that be obvious?" Michael peered at his wish-list again. "Aren't these things, stuff people would buy when they have money?"

"Yes, but at some point you run out of things to buy, and then your focus starts to shift. But the interesting thing is that the majority of the items you wanted to buy for yourself were opulent displays of wealth — such as fabulously expensive antique furniture, decorative items, items that show quite a bit of — bling," said Ian. "You only started considering things for your wife or kids when you ran out of buying choices."

"Ya, I think I am not a very good father and husband...." Michael started, eyes downcast.

"Whoa—whoa! This little game is not an excuse for you to beat yourself up, but to determine what your unconscious priorities were. It's an opportunity for you to truly understand that your beliefs even drive your spending habits!" Ian chipped in. "Most, if not all of the items you wanted for yourself were essentially material goods, stuff that proclaimed to the world, " I am rich, I have made it, Look at me with envy!""

Ian's expression then grew serious. "What this merely means is that your ego rather specifically, the need for validation of your success is more important than anything else. But remember all that talk about the *Universal Law of Attraction* that we hear so much about? What's the core principle?"

"Um....that we create our experience?" Michael answered hopefully.

"Exactly — and if we are the creators of our own experience and therefore happiness, what use have you for having a belief in needing validation and praise and therefore spending money buying things that you truly do not need merely to justify that belief?" pressed Ian. "Not only are you locked in an endless cycle of fuelling an unnecessary belief, you are trapped in a belief that does not serve you or the ones you love."

The mood grew somber as the weight of Ian's words sank into Michael's heart. "But does that mean buying stuff is not good? I like my Rolex watch, and the SUV I had before I was forced to sell it for money?" Michael felt overwhelmed by the sudden understanding of how his own belief system worked.

Ian ignored the bitterness in Michael's voice and pressed on. "Again, we need to realize that this exercise is not a means of judging what you buy, but also asking why you buy. When you realize now that it's your ego or the need for being recognized for your achievements is in fact the belief that's driving your actions, shouldn't you then be moving towards *Setting* better beliefs? You have had these current beliefs for many, many years; ask yourself, have you gotten any happier? Even at your most "prosperous", when you had a fair number of material wealth and stuff you liked, were you truly happy? Was the relationship between you and your family better?"

Michael pondered on Ian's question for many minutes. "I only remembered constantly looking for new hobbies or things to buy." He shook his head. "But I never had a single memory of being truly happy with my wife or family."

Ian straightened his posture and stood up. "Now you begin to truly understand the difference between acquiring money and attaining true happiness. It's easy to earn lots of money — but it's only an empty promise once you get these things. But that's old news isn't it?"

"What's critical now is the next step in *Setting* new beliefs and goals, now that the simple money game has confirmed what your *Sorting Board* has shown you. So what do you really want?" Ian asked.

"Well, I want to be a good father, and a good husband. I want to have a happy and joyous family," Michael murmured.

Ian beamed. "Good, because of the *Sorting Board*, and its findings and the link that is connected to your spending habits, you now realize that what you really want and what you were doing before does not match."

"Now then is the time to do some *Setting* of new goals and beliefs. With the need to be a better husband and father being your primary goals, you need to do some more homework — create a *Setting Board* where you place your new and positive goals and beliefs," explained Ian.

Michael watched as Ian sketched an example of the *Setting Board*. At that moment, he felt the need to start scribbling down his revised goals and beliefs. "What else do I need to do?"

"Well the *Setting Board* comes with a sister. It's called a *Vision Board,* Once you have outlined the positive beliefs and goals, you need to prove to yourself how it will be manifested. Nothing beats putting together words and pictures that are the end result of your beliefs and goals," Ian started to sketch another diagram furiously.

"The *Vision Board* is a very powerful exercise as it is a serious demonstration of how your beliefs and goals will manifest in its fullest. So if you choose to have a happy family relationship stated in your *Setting Board*, you would probably have a nice picture of a happy family taking a vacation somewhere in your *Vision Board,*" Ian explained.

"It's going to take some work. I don't even dare to think what I want because it may be just my ego," lamented Michael.

"Don't worry," assured Ian. "You won't, as you have made your new beliefs and goals clearly in your *Setting Board*. The beauty of what we are doing here is that this process allows you to move backwards and forwards in this process when you are aligned with your beliefs."

Michael left Ian's home that evening feeling at once heavy-hearted but hopeful. "How did I get into this cycle so badly and never realized it?" he thought, as he gunned his car engine. "More importantly, can I ever break free from this cycle and take affirmative action and see results?" That night held no answers for Michael.

Points to ponder

Things started to get really serious and tense once the Sorting Board exercise has started. It is perfectly natural as the Sorting Board unveils many hidden beliefs — and negative ones at that. The key is to maintain an attitude of learning and discovering, and giving yourself permission to observe what you have been doing and unlearning these beliefs.

One useful checkpoint demonstrated was the use of a simple game which allowed both Michael and Ian to get a sense of how Michael's belief systems were controlling his habit of spending. The simple game's results were an infallible indication of the truths unveiled in the Sorting Board about Michael's core weakness.

The next step is to create a Setting Board which is an exercise in committing to creating new beliefs that replace the negative ones identified previously. This is followed by creating a Vision Board that further commits your beliefs into visuals and pictures that represent the end goals.

Each step has to be done as part of the Living Kaizen process as it gives the person time to feel and time to recover. It is also a failsafe option that should the negative beliefs and feelings released by the affirmative statements not succeed, the Setting and Vision Board will create the space for healing to take place.

MICHAEL'S SETTING BOARD

CREATIVE

PERSEVERENCE / PATIENCE

PASSIONATE ABOUT HELPING PEOPLE

CAREFUL / METICULOUS

NOT ANALYTICAL ⟶ ANALYTICAL

CARE FOR THE FAMILY

STUBBORN ⟶ ADAPTABLE

STRONG WILLED ⟶ FLEXIBLE BUT WITH STRONG VALUES

CONSERVATIVE ⟶ OPEN MINDED AND WILLING TO EXPLORE NEW THINGS & NEW IDEAS

LECTURER MINDED ⟶ SPEAK WITH THE TRUTH WITH COMPASSION

EMOTIONALLY UNSTABLE ⟶ PEACE OF MIND AND JOYFUL

NOT CLOSE TO FAMILY ⟶ LOVING & CONSIDERATE & UNDERSTANDING

JUSTIFYING WITH EXCUSES ⟶ TAKING RESPONSIBILITY

BLAME SITUATION ON OTHERS ⟶ TAKING RESPONSIBILITY

Michael's Vision Board

Living Kaizen to sell a million copies

European Cruise (5-star) with wife

Bungalow with 10,000 sq.

Living Kaizen session to a crowd of 5,000

Donate 4 dialysis Machines

COV

Holidays with wife & 2 children.

Chapter 4 — Shining like a beacon in the dark...

It was another 2 weeks before Michael could manage to meet up with Ian. During those 2 weeks, Michael had pondered about his weaknesses and his past beliefs. In quiet anticipation, he also prepared both his *Setting* and *Vision Board* but did not have any idea how to go about it.

So it was with some urgency that he finally met Ian. "Sorry, I couldn't meet up with you earlier," apologized Ian while pulling up his chair.

Michael shook his head. "I was really trying to figure out how to go about doing this."

He showed his *Sorting* and *Vision Board* to Ian. Ian looked at the two boards, nodding his head in approval.

"Good stuff you did Michael. There's really a distinctive link between your old beliefs and the transformation into new ones in your *Setting Board*. I see that your *Vision Board* is just as meticulously done," said Ian with quiet approval.

"But that's the point, you see," began Michael. "For the last two weeks, I knew what I had to change and do — but I don't know exactly how to go about doing it."

"It's all fine and dandy for gurus out there to talk about a concept of change — but I believe I need something a bit more process-driven. Even in my training sessions at factories, I find that a step-by-step process works better as it's easier to follow something rather than leaving it to imagination," Michael added.

"I see what you mean — which is why we need an action plan that will help you *Shine* in your practice of creating what you want with your new beliefs and goals," Ian said, pulling out a clean sheet of paper. "The beauty of *Living Kaizen* is that what is seen as to *Shine* in the task is a metaphor for taking action and doing things that measure up to all that you have prepared in *Sorting* and *Setting*."

"The action plan requires you to understand and internalize two principles," Ian continued. "The first thing you need to know is that *Belief* creates *Attitudes, Attitudes* create *Behaviour*, and *Behaviour* creates *Results*," he said, drawing a simple diagram illustrating his words.

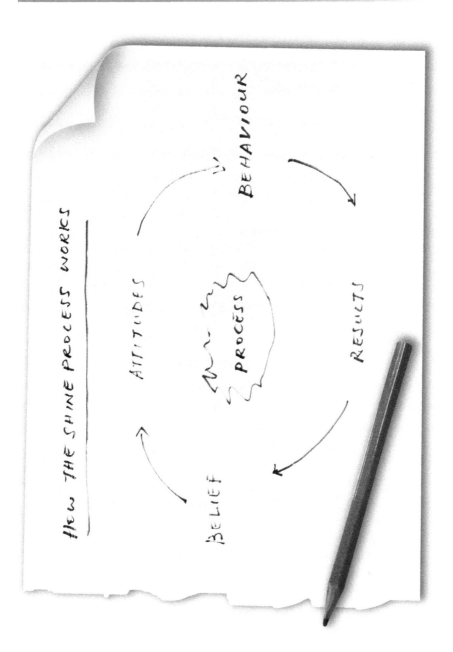

HOW THE SHINE PROCESS WORKS

BEHAVIOUR

ATTITUDES

PROCESS

RESULTS

BELIEF

"Everything you do from now on will fundamentally change because you know that it's merely an end product of your beliefs," Ian explained. "The next thing you need to know is that it takes practice, practice, practice."

"Practice?" Michael queried.

"Yup, practice. Did you know that it takes 28 days of constant "doing" something for the brain to recognize it as a new task and create new neurological impulses?" Ian started to draw up a list.

"Really?" Michael was surprised.

"And the process in which I will share with you will require you to practice it everyday for the next 28 days until it's second nature to you," replied Ian with a glint in his eye, as he finished up his list.

"We call this portion the *Shining Process* — in honour of the fact that when you have mastery over this process, there will be nothing that you cannot do, no dreams you cannot materialize, no goal that you cannot achieve and no challenge you cannot overcome," Ian unveiled his handiwork with relish.

Michael blinked at Ian's crude handwriting for several moments trying to understand the ramifications of the list.

"Here, let me tell you what you need to do," Ian quickly added, snatching up the paper filled with diagrams.

"Once you have mastery over this, you will require very minimal effort to manage your day-to-day life as well as control your beliefs and behaviour. But for every process, you must first attune yourself to the right vibration — and the best mood to be in when we start this process is to have the attitude of *Gratitude*," Ian pointed to the first phrase.

"Every morning when you wake up, master the art of beginning your day with thoughts of gratitude. You may want to be grateful for being where you are, for having a roof over your head, the love and support of the wife sleeping next to you etc. The objective is to truly feel the feelings of gratitude, real gratitude and enjoy these feelings for about ten minutes."

Ian narrowed his eyes. "The disclaimer is that you must feel it, and not just think about it without any feeling attached to it. Make sure you have a list somewhere of the things you are grateful for. It's always good to start of by saying, "I am so very happy and grateful for…" and then putting down the things you feel gratitude in having."

"Once you have spent some time feeling grateful for the things you have, it's time to get up from bed and before you even go to the bathroom, you need to focus on your *Vision Board*," Ian continued. "Remember all the nice pictures and words you put into your board? That board plays a very important role here. Spend time looking at each of the things you have put up on that board and generate the feelings of having done that already."

"Wait a minute — actually pretend I already have those?" Michael asked, "Wouldn't that be like deceiving myself?"

"The purpose of feeling it runs in line with our understanding in the *Universal Law of Attraction*," assured Ian. "The mind cannot discern what is real and what is not. It doesn't matter that you do not possess that car or that house. What matters is that you can create the feelings of joy and happiness owning those things can do for you."

"So spend some time going through your *Vision Board* and generate those joyful, happy feelings of having achieved those goals. Then on the same wave of feelings, go through a mental list of the things you will do well and excel for the next 24 hours," Ian finished with a beatific smile.

"Mental list?" Michael mused, "Sort of like an action list — right?"

"Exactly!" replied Ian triumphantly. "Prepare this mental list of things you want to do with regards to what you have highlighted in your *Setting Board*. For example, your *Setting Board* revealed that you truly wanted a more fulfilling relationship with your wife and children. You can be well on your way to making that a reality by giving your wife and kids a hug and a kiss everyday and telling them you love them very much."

"I see what you mean, so I can have this mental list that I can put to-do things that matter to my goals and dreams," said Michael enthusiastically. "What about my work? Can I put in a to-do list of things that matter to me at work, such as completing that deal with a client on a positive note?"

"Absolutely! Now you are getting the hang of it!" Ian whooped, giving Michael a big pat on his back. "The best part about this mental list is that it also works on your bad habits too."

"You know that you shouldn't drink so much, right? But it's not about the drinking but more about the companionship with your friends and that's how you found out in your *Sorting Board*.

So in your *Setting Board*, you wanted to drink less and be healthier. So why not put that in your mental list? Instead of having 4 beers today after work, visualize and feel how satisfied you would be having only 2 beers and then going home earlier to spend some quality time with your wife and kids?"

"Hmmm, this could work," mused Michael thinking about his beers.

"Once you got that list, you need to feel what it's like completing those tasks easily," continued Ian.

"After you have freshened up and ready to go, you need to *Energize* your day," Ian pointed to the 4th step in the chart.

"How do I energize my day apart from a nice cup of coffee and already being in a state of mind of pure positive energy? What else do I need?" Michael was puzzled.

"Remember one mini-exercise I asked you to do the last time we met? It was about remembering 10 of your favourite songs?" Ian asked with a grin.

"Oh yeah, I do — I picked ten songs that made me feel good - oh I get it!" Michael exclaimed. "If I get into my car and picked any of my ten favourite songs to listen to, I would almost guarantee that I will feel good driving to my next appointment!"

"Excellent! Now *Energizing* yourself can be more than just listening to your favourite songs, it could also mean capturing a moment of your greatest happiness and joy and locking it with a special word or behaviour," said Ian. "For example, if you took some time to remember an event where you felt the most confident

— say the time you closed the biggest sale, you could hang on to that thought and locked it in with a power move — making a fist and going "Yes!" or some bodily action that you wouldn't normally do but would remember doing it," Ian demonstrated. Michael immediately noticed the sudden physiological change once Ian activated his anchor.

"The best thing is that when you start to feel down and out, all you have to do is *Energize* yourself using any of the things you've learnt from music to creating physical anchors and you have a ready supply of positive energy on tap all the time!"

Ian took a deep breath and let it out slowly. "It is almost always true that at some point or other during the day, we may be faced with an unexpected situation that is negative or creates negativity in our hearts. The *Shining Process* recognizes this as contrast — or events that are in contrast to what you would like to have. It could be as simple as having gotten a flat tyre, or meeting someone unpleasant who dislikes you — anything as long as it succeeded in putting you in a state of mind that's negative and makes you feel bad."

"*Living Kaizen* sees this as contrast — nothing more — and how you manage it in the *Shining Process* is to acknowledge the experience as contrast, and very quickly finding the opposite positive experience to that. For example, if meeting an unpleasant person in your sales pitch is the contrasting experience, then recognize that as an experience you do not wish to have, and then visualize meeting a person that was very enthusiastic and helpful to generate the feelings of how good it would be meeting that person," Ian said.

"This step of *Reviewing Contrast* leads then to the process of *Re-visualizing* positive experiences — directly opposite of that contrasting experience. It may seem like a mouthful, but it always guarantees that you end your day on a very positive note! Because when you *Re-visualize*, you are already setting the tone and vibration in determining how positive you will be feeling the next day!" Ian declared.

Michael gazed at Ian's drawings in silence, letting his words sink in. "It's finally a step-by-step process I can refer to every time," said Michael. Confidence blossomed within as Michael began to realize the effect this process would have on his day-to-day experience.

"It's easy and yet so effective! I must begin doing it!" said Michael with hope in his heart.

"Remember it takes practice and practice," admonished Ian. "Keep doing that everyday for the next 28 days and I guarantee you something is going to happen within you that will fundamentally change the way you look at each day and experience."

Michael left Ian's place that night full of anticipation and excitement. Finally, he was able to pro-actively move towards changing his life. Michael wondered how much of what he had learnt that night will impact the world around him. Time would tell.

Points to ponder

Michael had indeed reached a new point of action in his life. That night, Ian revealed the action keys that would take all that Michael learnt into practice. The Shining Process, gleefully revealed action steps that Michael could take every day so he could put into practice what he Sort, Set and put in his Vision Boards.

In the following diagrams, Ian outlined in great detail, how Michael could leverage on the step-by-step process and create a habit or behaviour of attuning himself towards fulfilling what he wanted to achieve for that day. The Shining Process is comprehensive in ensuring that challenges or issues that were experienced during the day would be pro-actively managed and remolded into a positive learning and projecting experience.

Michael left realizing that this was indeed a point of no return as he had the right tools to begin transforming his life.

SHINE PROCESS

STEP 1 — GRATITUDE

STEP 2 — VISUALISE

STEP 3 — ACTION POINTS

STEP 4 — ENERGISE

STEP 5 — REVIEW CONTRAST

STEP 6 — REVISUALISE

STEP 1 - GRATITUDE

I am grateful and now that I have

A very comfortable & nice house to provide me
shelter

My beautiful wife & lovely children are healthy

The learning experiences of life I have gone through

The up & growing business which is propelling
me to prosperity

The people I met who guided me through their
advice & encouragement which is helping me
to achieve my success.

STEP 2 — VISUALISE

1. Look into the vision / manifestation board.

2. Think about the things you have in the vision board.

3. Feel the feelings of joy you already have in the vision / manifestation board

4. Spend 2 minutes feeling the joy of achieving each particular item on the vision / manifestation board.

STEP 3 — ACTION POINTS

- Meet headmasters/headmistress of 7 targeted schools and achieve 100% success and achieve

- Follow up on 6 past contacts and achieve breakthrough results

- Getting my children to & from school and tuition classes with plenty of time to spare with no jams

- Helping my children with their homework easily and effectively

- Exercise well by walking around my neighbourhood 3 times with my dog

- Spend 1 hour with my wife actively listening to her talking about her day

- Help my wife solve any pending issues at home or at work decisively within 1 hour

STEP 4 - ENERGISE YOUR DAY

Create things to do or listen that gives me
joy and happiness or puts me in a positive
mood.

- Listen to 10 most favourable songs

- Pick, store and read 10 most empowering
  statements

- Lock down a gesture that reminds me of
  the most successful and happiest moment
  in my life

STEP 5 — REVIEW CONTRAST

Log down the negative experiences of the day to be reviewed, acknowledged and if necessary to Re-Sort and Re-Set

Review Contrast

1. Failing to make a good impression on the principal of one of the schools

2. Delay the appointment with client because forgot to bring along the documents

3. Scolded daughter for failing to meet at designated place on time

4. Scolded my wife for not coming home on time

5. Failure to maintain positive attitude after a few unsuccessful meetings

6. Impatience & frustration when waiting to meet with school principal

Re-Sort

1. Disappoint and angry at myself →

2. → Shame →

3. failing→frustrated & resentment →

4. → hurt and betrayed →

5. → fear of continuing failure →

6. → fear of not being recognised or respected →

Releasing

I release to feel disappointed and angry at myself

ashamed of myself

frustrated and resentful

hurt and betrayed

fear of continuing failure

fear of not being recognised and respected

These feelings do not serve me.

I release these feelings now.
So be it.

STEP 6 – REVISUALISE

Based on what you have Re-Sorted and released from your contrasting experiences. Re-Set / Revisualise the new experiences in a positive manner and choose to feel the feelings of success, happiness and satisfaction.

Review Contrast		Re-Set / Revisualise
1. Failing to make a good impression on the school principal	→	Committing to and succeeding in making a powerful, positive impact in every meeting.
2. Delay the appointment with client because forgot to bring along documents	→	Committing to and succeeding in being well prepared and being early for meetings and presentations.
3. Scolded daughter for failing to meet at designated place on time	→	Be compassionate and seek to clarify any issue with my daughters and resolve them in a positive manner.
4. Scolded my wife for not coming home on time	→	Be understanding and compassionate with my wife at all times.
5. Failure to maintain positive attitude after a few unsuccessful meetings	→	Always be in a constant state of joy and gratitude and be committed to improve myself at every meeting.
6. Impatience & frustration when waiting to meet school principal	→	Choose to feel gratitude at having the chance to share my life purpose with people despite time constraints

Chapter 5 — Sustaining the faith

The weeks that followed for Michael become the true turning point in his life. Armed with a step-by-step discipline, he dutifully followed the *Shine* process meticulously, and began to manifest events and experiences quite different from what he was used to.

The most obvious manifestation of change was in his work. Schools and institutions that Michael approached previously but had no success became renewed possibilities for him. Strengthened by what he knew was his life purpose, Michael re-approached his old list of contacts and possible clients. Amazingly, doors which were closed on him previously, suddenly began to open. Schools started buying his training posters, while some even wanted him to present his Kaizen principles to school assemblies for children. Small and medium sized companies started returning his calls with intent to find out more and purchase not only his posters but his training courses. Before long, Michael was busier than he ever was before!

There was an even bigger surprise for Michael — and this was at home.

His wife and children became noticeably more communicative and closer to him, especially in their weekly routine family activities. Michael noticed this with great excitement, for he also realized that he was creating the environment he wanted in his *Living Kaizen* process. During this period of time he kept in touch with Ian via sms and short telephone conversations. The wave of change was happening in his life and he was participating fully and with great passion in it.

During those fateful weeks, Michael discovered a hidden strength and wisdom he never knew he had. It was as if everything happened for a reason, and that things were well within his control and mastery. When a problem occurred, Michael was quick to assess the possible reasons of his own thinking and actions, instead of finding excuses or laying blame before. This subtle yet dynamic change in his attitude surprised even his wife, who had been quite convinced that her husband was incurable in his ways. Although things were looking up, she was still worrying obsessively over the probability of his success. Michael's astonishing display and practice of being energetic, positive and determination had put her in a quandary. It worried her so much, she started to lose her hair. Michael, who did his share of the housework, noticed it.

When he checked with Ian over the phone, Ian broke into gales of laughter. "I think it's amazing that your wife is suitably impressed by your turnaround to lose hair over it!" Ian guffawed. "I gave my wife the assurance that all will be well — but I guess I still need to continue to work on that area in terms of giving her the peace of mind." Michael noted wryly.

"Yup! And once it manifests, your family will be more than surprised by the new and improved Michael — you just got to give them some time to adjust to you," Ian enthused. "So go out there and make it happen!"

With the new rhythm of his energy in place, Michael filled his weeks with a myriad experiences in success and new—found peace in his heart as he went about fulfilling his purpose of sharing his systems and practices with others.

However, it was a number of weeks which Michael had not seen Ian. There were many days in which, he barely answered Michael's short messages and phone calls.

But something started to happen during those weeks.

The feeling was subtle.

The effect was insidious...

The realization of it over time was quite worrisome.

When Ian answered Michael's latest call some weeks after, Michael discovered a worry that he wanted to share. Ian agreed to set up their long delayed meeting.

"So, how's it been?" asked Ian when he ushered Michael in.

"Ya — ya...everything seems to be moving in the right direction. My business is picking up at a rate I never dreamt possible. And the energy and purpose which I have is bonding my family closer than ever." Michael said.

"But....?"

Ian peered at Michael expectantly as he fidgeted in his seat.

"I discovered a glitch in this process — and while I realize that it has done absolutely wonders for me, I missed the sessions we had when we were analyzing and taking steps to move forward. It's all there, yet I felt increasingly lethargic during certain times, and even notice my excuses coming back into my thoughts," Michael blurted out.

"So in other words, you worry you are caught in a rut and that you aren't *Sustaining the Sort, Set & Shine Process*?" teased Ian with a grin on his face.

"Precisely," Michael exhaled, rolling his eyes upward. "I cannot expect you to be my always-available-ever-ready coach that can give me a shot in the arm —"

"— or a kick in the butt," quipped Ian.

" — or a kick in the butt on demand can I?" Michael continued. "I mean it has been terrible trying to meet up with you, especially you being busy and all. While I know it's got everything to do with me, how do I know that I am still *Living Kaizen*?"

"That's probably the most difficult part of *Living Kaizen*." Ian replied sipping his tea. "In every aspect of life, sustaining progress, hope or positive energy is perhaps the most challenging, in the best of circumstances. But it is critical to believe that these ruts exist as proof of the "BIG-ness" of change or improvement that we are going through."

"So, is the first step to acknowledge the ruts I face as proof that I am on the right track?" Michael asked, leaning forward.

"Yes. These contrasts, or ruts or challenges are indications that while you are headed in the right direction, you need to make constant adjustments to keep your journey steady and true. But knowing it is not enough as you say, there needs to be a way to truly know that you are on the right path to *Shining* in what you have *Set* out to do." Ian explained.

"One perfect gauge is to use your *emotions*."

"Emotions? Aren't we supposed to be rational human beings, not given to our baser instincts such as emotions?" Michael was very skeptical.

"The thing is at our very core, we are emotional beings, without which we wouldn't be human after all," Ian responded. "What we need to learn in order to *Sustain Living Kaizen* is to *Observe* very carefully our state of emotions and mind."

"From the perspective of *Living Kaizen*, we simply put them either as good, or not good. Every emotion we experience falls into either good or not good categories," said Ian. "For example, for us human beings, what's the best thing to feel good about is to feel joy. The least emotion we don't feel so good about is despair. So the fact is you coming here and sharing your concerns with me has resulted in you feeling...."

"Good? Yeah, I feel better talking to you," Michael remarked, finishing Ian's sentence.

"That's right. By recognizing that you felt not so good when you were in the rut was a clear indication that you needed to adjust your course of action," explained Ian. "The beauty of your emotions is that emotions don't lie. Our higher consciousness lies, justifies and lays blame — never our emotions. You did not feel good, you listened to your emotions, and you practiced *Living*

Kaizen by acting on what you felt would make you feel better," Ian replied.

Ian was on to something here, and Michael could feel it.

"So our emotions guide our well-being," Michael said.

"Yes, absolutely! To *Sustain Living Kaizen* we must re-connect with our emotions," exclaimed Ian.

"Reconnecting with our emotions mean that we must be able to *Observe* and know which emotional level we are at any particular moment. Spend a moment *Recognizing* the emotion you are feeling. Knowing this means we are able to place precisely how we are feeling," said Ian. "*Living Kaizen* isn't about miracles, but continuous improvements, so if you have observed that you are feeling angry, take a moment to recognize that. Then *Adjust* your level of emotion and choose to *Feel* an emotion which is a step better than anger, say resentment. Spend a few moments feeling resentment. *Observing* you feeling the resentment and *Recognize* that it is a step forward toward feeling good. Then *Adjust*."

"I get it!" Michael exclaimed. "While the *Sorting*, *Setting* and *Shining* are the main moving parts in *Living Kaizen* that helps me to improve my life, *Sustaining* the faith by being aware and in-touch with my emotions gives me the fine-tuning skills I need to continue to stay in that positive state of heart and mind."

"And that is how *Living Kaizen* is so infinitely useful!" Ian was grinning like a Cheshire cat. "Its processes and disciplines make use of both conscious and sub-conscious parts of you, recognizing for you to truly *Live* in a *Kaizen* way, rational and emotional portions must constantly be at work — achieving a balance that is complex when revealed, but oh so simple when practiced."

The room felt charged with energy as Michael digested the ramifications of *Living Kaizen*.

"*Sustaining* the *Faith* requires you to *Observe, Recognize, Adjust* and *Feel*. Practice that every time you feel doubt, when you are stuck in a rut, or when you just don't know if you are on the right track in line with *Sorting, Setting, Shining* your way to happiness," Ian said softly.

"How do you feel?"

"Like getting a free "get out of trouble" card in my favourite board game," said Michael. "I have now a clear and easy way of using my emotions as radar to check on myself as I move on pursuing my life purpose."

"Liberating isn't it?" Ian smiled, drawing their meeting to a close.

 Points to ponder

At some point in our pursuit of happiness and growth, we will come across contrasting situations, like being in a rut, caught in a moment of indecision, or fear. Living Kaizen recognizes these situations as events and experiences that test the faith, and has in its practice a fool-proof method of Sustaining the faith.

Sustaining the faith in its essence leverages on a person's connection or re-connection to his or her emotions. Not only is knowledge and awareness of one's emotions necessary, it is also critical that one is able to learn how to observe one's own state of emotion at any time. The Sustaining factor of Living Kaizen follows a 4-step principle, namely Observe, Recognize, Adjust and Feel.

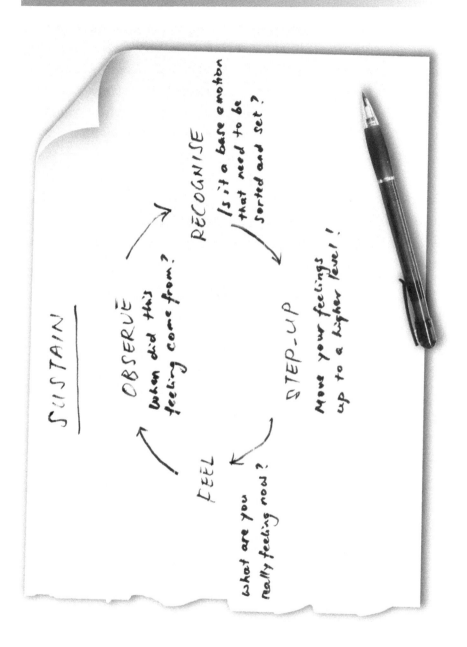

At any point in practicing Living Kaizen, Sustaining is a powerful component is self-assessment and self-correction while pursuing one's dreams and desires. It is a powerful watchdog in preventing the more subtle nuances of negative thinking to seep into the heart and mind. Emotions do not lie, but the mind unfortunately does. Hence, Sustaining leverages on the person's emotional scale as a means of re-calibrating and counter-checking on the mind. For those who are truly curious, the complexities of the mind-body-emotion can be far better explained in more specialized books and topics, but the implications of this relationship and the means of getting emotions to work for us are far-reaching and powerful beyond measure.

"In the face of adversity, you will face your greatest challenge — You." — Iihann

Chapter 6 — Know your Self

That night at Ian's house provided Michael with renewed vigor and determination in pursuing his goals and dreams. The *Sustain* discipline allowed Michael to begin appreciating the power of his emotions. The knowledge that everyone was imbued with their own individual emotional guidance gave Michael the perfect fallback to check upon his progress and his state of heart and mind.

Michael set himself back to his work with renewed zest and peace of mind.

Weeks passed and results began to manifest.

Deals from different clients began to manifest. Michael noted that for as long as he followed the process in *Living Kaizen*, his days began to flow smoothly, easily and successfully. Expanding his business scope, he began to move into government institutions, city councils, ministries and even universities, all with amazing results. With each visit, Michael would leave his business card and a leaflet behind explaining his life purpose and that of his work. Where previously he would visit prospects dressed in whichever he could find, he started applying *Living Kaizen* principles to his dress code and conduct. In no time he began to realize that even his dressing style began to reflect the positive and exuberant energy that he felt and manifested. Prospects started to respond positively to his first contact meetings, something which he never experienced previously.

"Something truly amazing is definitely happening. I was never so warmly received by new clients before," thought Michael after a particularly successful meeting.

With a clearer mind, Michael began to regain skills and ideas which he never thought he had before. Ways of marketing his posters and his consulting services began to fill his mind. These ideas were quickly put to use, further enriching his business cycle. His waking hours were now filled with result-orientated actions and forward thinking plans.

Perhaps the most telling change Michael manifested was in his financial management. Previously he would use his old Kaizen skills to dispose of his assets as a means of managing finances, often seeing it as useful tool in helping him out of situations. However, practising *Living Kaizen* allowed him to view his finances differently. Michael began to realize that his previous (indeed almost as if it was his past life — because it's changed so much!) view of finances were bogged down in insecurity and feelings of scarcity, forever perpetuating an environment of hopelessness and guilt.

Where before there was lack, he now saw amazing opportunities for leverage, and of support. Practicing *Living Kaizen* gave Michael tremendous advantage in seeing issues as merely answers and solutions waiting to happen. Likewise, this change of mindset turned his finances around. Where previously he was afraid to spend money in certain necessities like repairing his old car, using *Living Kaizen* allowed him to realize that spending it was important as it made his work far more comfortable, and helping anchor his positive mood during his sales trips.

Michael used to see banks as sharks, due to his experience in debt. Practising *Living Kaizen*'s principles allowed him to resolve his insecurities in asking for financial support from banks — freeing not only his limiting beliefs, but empowering him to leverage on these financial behemoths. In no time at all, he was able to dramatically slash his debts by brokering a loan from the bank and creating an automatic loan-repayment scheme which allowed him greater mastery on his overall financial portfolio. This shift in mindset allowed him to manage his assets with greater finesse — further netting him profit.

It was great having money in his pocket again. The amount was of no consequence. It was the feeling of gratitude and joy in having money that made Michael happy.

Friends and relatives, who were used to giving Michael lectures on money and personal management, started to notice the spring in Michael's step, his upright posture and even his manner and behaviour.

"Eh, is your husband alright? He won the lottery and never told us did he? What's he so happy and positive about? Share market dropped 10 points today you know," they would whisper to his wife. Alas, the poor woman had no answer to give, although she secretly hoped that this wonderful behaviour would continue.

Michael's success started to radiate benefits towards his family. Because *Living Kaizen* gave him the discipline to create the environment and the experience, Michael could even spend quality time with his family every day, even with his busy schedule. During those times, Michael would often reflect on his past, noting that in times past, he would waste his hours either at the local pub or be cooped up in his room, listless and despondent at the lack of success. Michael's wife noted that he even seemed to enjoy doing house chores, often whistling a merry tune bustling about the home and cheerfully completing tasks which she would normally do. How strange and wonderful this sudden turn of events are!

One day, Michael was waiting for an appointment with a chief purchasing officer who had called to enquire about the Kaizen posters for a private manufacturing company. This was a fantastic opportunity for Michael to introduce *Living Kaizen* (no more was it just plain old Kaizen now!) to more than 600 workers.

After ten minutes, he was ushered into a plush office. The officer was behind his desk and motioned for Michael to take a seat. Michael proceeded to share his work and the posters to the officer who seemed distracted. In due time talk turned to the costings of the posters. The officer immediately became attentive. After Michael highlighted the costings, the officer spoke.

"I think your posters are good, and I would like to order a batch from you. However, I would like you to do something beneficial for me — ah, as a gesture of your goodwill," the officer said pointedly, toying with a gold-chased calculator on his table.

Michael was nonplussed. "Sir, may I ask for clarification as to what you mean by gesture of goodwill?" In his mind, Michael was wondering if the officer wanted a complimentary training session for his staff or a free poster.

"Aaah, you know. All you have to do is mark up the poster cost and do something beneficial for me with the difference," The officer seemed annoyed by Michael's ignorance.

"But sir, my posters are fixed priced," blurted Michael. What was this guy talking about?

"Ok, let me put it plainly — what's my commission for buying your posters?"

The officer's tone turned ominous, as he eyed Michael with furrowed brow and slitted eye.

Michael was in a quandary. "I — I will need to talk to my boss and get back to you on this," he stammered, drawing the meeting to a close. Michael left the office feeling somewhat tainted by the experience. During his drive home, he decided to pay Ian a surprise visit.

It was late in the evening when Ian helped himself and Michael to a cup of tea each. "You look pissed. What happened?" Ian asked taking an appreciative sip of oolong tea.

Michael gulped his tea in silence, trying to remember the specifics. In short terse sentences, he related the incident to Ian, who continued sipping his tea. When he finished, Ian looked thoughtful.

"Did you practice *Sort* and *Set* on this issue as we discussed?" Ian asked quietly.

"The thing is, I know that I was exposed to this type of corruption early in my life — it's no different than being swindled," declared Michael vehemently. "But being literally put in that situation especially when selling those posters profitably made me feel dirty all over. I just wanted to tell him to stick his head up you know where and storm out of the office."

"We both know graft is prevalent in our world — but the context of this incident — especially when you are doing so well in your life is a stark contrasting experience," Ian said, pouring himself another cup of tea. "It's an indication that while you find yourself, you will need to make hard decisions — some of which will impact your business bottom line, or your conscience."

"I will not support corruption," Michael declared.

"Commendable, but there's more to it than just deciding based on this," Ian cautioned. "There will be many more such contrasting events in the future that will test you on other values. There will be times when the line between black and white isn't as simple."

Silence sank like a blanket while Michael pondered upon what Ian said. "It's all about how I choose my moral and ethical values isn't it?"

"Yes," replied Ian. "The *Sort, Set, Shine* and *Sustain* portions of *Living Kaizen* makes us better people all round — but what they cannot do is define our value systems. It does however promise to set events in motion that will inevitably raise the issue, as you re-create your life experience. Events and people you meet will conspire to test your moral and ethical anchors. For without these anchors, you are not able to achieve progress, nor chart your happiness with clarity."

"Which is why the 5th discipline of *Living Kaizen* is applied, which is achieving *Self-Values*," Ian revealed. "And this involves you doing a moral and ethical audit on yourself."

"But how do I do that without letting my conscious side make excuses or justifications? It would be an exercise in self-deception,"

Michael said, worry playing across his face. "Goodness knows I have faced that before during my *Sorting* and *Setting* stages."

"Which is why the audit involves simple muscle testing," replied Ian. "I need you to come up with a list which encompasses the moral and ethical values you think you would want to have. Once you have that list, I need you to stand up."

Stand up? This was something very new! Michael quickly drew up a list of more than 20 moral values that he thought he would like. Passing the list to Ian who scanned it quickly, Michael stood up.

"Ok, I need you to relax your posture, keeping your feet close together and facing forward. Got it?" Ian instructed. Michael did as was instructed and relaxed his posture.

"Now I need you to raise your right hand and put it to your heart. Good. Now the first value on your list is honesty, right? Now in your current posture, ask yourself this — do I want to live my life with honest values?" Ian prompted.

Michael closed his eyes and asked the question out loud. Strangely enough, he felt his body started to sway forward. Catching himself quickly he turned towards Ian with questing eyes.

"Excellent. Did you notice you unconsciously leaned forward? That is your subconscious *Self* answering the statement for you. If your body leans forward unconsciously, it means that your inner wisdom is in complete agreement with you," Ian explained.

"Let's try something different. Try to pick a value not in the list — say "I want to take advantage of any situation," said Ian.

"That's a vague statement — but ok." Michael tried it. To his utter surprise, his body reared back unexpectedly, nearly making him fall backwards.

"What the hell just happened?" Michael gasped, quickly sitting down.

"That was your inner wisdom completely disagreeing with what you just wanted to do," replied Ian. "It's a simple muscle test — and works on the principle far more obvious and just as accurately as the emotional guidance scale in *Sustain*. Your inner wisdom and your emotions do not lie — and doing this test is the sure-fire way to anchor down your values."

"Now all you got to do is go home and run through that list, using a full-length mirror so you can see yourself peripherally to double-check whether you are leaning forward or backward. Remember, you must be relaxed and in an upright standing postition. Oh and don't let your mind wander except on that moral value you want to practice." Ian advised.

 Points to ponder

We are often faced with moral and ethical dilemmas in our life experience. Understanding them as contrasts that guide our way may point us to better direction, but until we choose to anchor our moral values, we would be confused. Michael faced the same dilemma in this chapter.

However, Living Kaizen leverages on simple yet effective muscle testing to aid in determining our moral compass. There are 2 stages to finding Self-Values in Living Kaizen. The first is to draw up a list of moral and ethical values that you think would matter.

Once you draw up the list, adopt the posture as shown and in a simple and methodical manner, ask yourself to adopt this value, keeping your mind focused only on the question. It's a universal sign that what your inner wisdom wants, it leans forward, but what it does not accept, it shies away from.

This exercise requires some practice, especially in relaxing your body enough to let its inner wisdom come through.

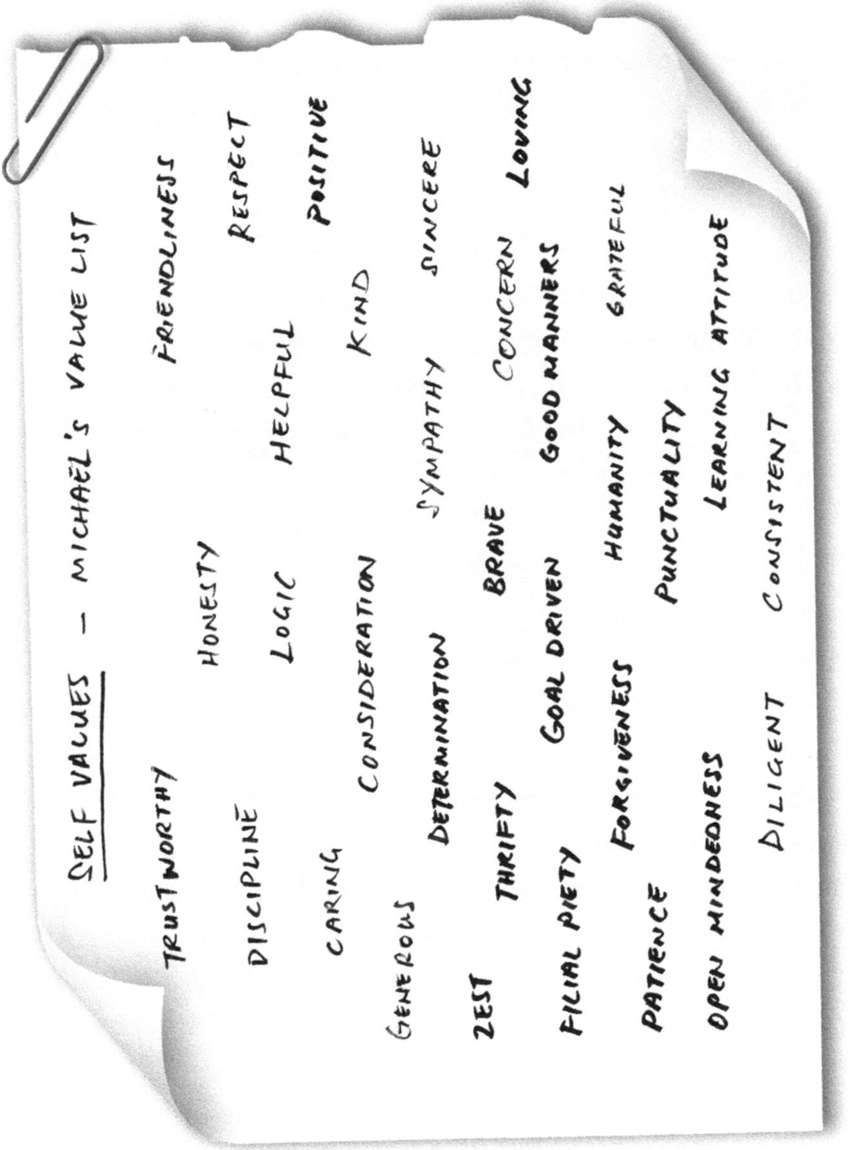

SELF VALUES — MICHAEL'S VALUE LIST

TRUSTWORTHY

HONESTY

FRIENDLINESS

RESPECT

DISCIPLINE

LOGIC

HELPFUL

POSITIVE

CARING

KIND

CONSIDERATION

GENEROUS

DETERMINATION

SYMPATHY

SINCERE

ZEST

THRIFTY

BRAVE

CONCERN

LOVING

FILIAL PIETY

GOAL DRIVEN

GOOD MANNERS

FORGIVENESS

HUMANITY

GRATEFUL

PATIENCE

PUNCTUALITY

OPEN MINDEDNESS

LEARNING ATTITUDE

DILIGENT

CONSISTENT

"*Values make powerful tools in helping you define your life purpose, but poor weapons if you use them to beat up another person.*"
— *Iihann*

Over the next few weeks, Michael spent many, many hours rediscovering his moral and ethical values. Applying the simple art of muscle testing, he was amazed at the clarity of his inner wisdom and its ability to decide which value best suited him.

Out of a myriad probable values that he thought he should have, Michael's inner wisdom revealed four particular ones that resonated deep within. Armed with his key values, Michael once again reapplied his knowledge and experience into his work.

He prospered.

Now Michael knew that success was inevitably his — by the fact that it no longer mattered how he justified his success by. It was the level of joy and happiness and satisfaction that became all that mattered. Where thoughts of potential failure used to be his every thought, he unconsciously began to visualize success, applying all the principles he had learnt in *Living Kaizen* to stay within his most positive state of mind.

Every night, before he went to bed, Michael would again complete his *Living Kaizen* exercises, and then re-look at the 4 values his inner wisdom so mysteriously revealed, pondering on its implications.

Something was eluding him. He sensed that those 4 values were meant to be more than just words that were picked out by his heart. He called Ian to ask about it.

"So you said in your audit, you had 4 very powerfully strong values picked out?" Ian asked.

"Yes, I did — they were *Discipline*, *Consideration*, *Logic* and *Friendliness*." replied Michael. "While the muscle-testing was an amazing experience for me, I felt that these 4 values meant something more than just the meanings from the dictionary," he explained.

"You are absolutely correct. These four words are just — words…nothing more," Ian said. "The challenge is for you in applying *Living Kaizen* to figure out the essence of these words and discover the depth and breadth that are within them."

Half-an-hour later, Michael felt even more confused. His phone call with Ian only added to his increasing worry about the hidden reasons behind these 4 seemingly innocent-looking values. Michael realized that he needed to persevere, while internalizing and practicing *Living Kaizen* in his life. Ian shared some stories, metaphors based on his experience of those values, but their significance were lost on Michael. But Michael knew that these things took some time, and patiently settled into living his life — the *Living Kaizen* way.

Discipline

The first indication that his patience was bearing fruit came surprisingly not through his work but in the dynamics of his relationship with his family. For many years, Michael viewed the workings of his own family with a mixture of detachment and distaste, often dealing out tongue-lashings on behaviour which he found intolerable. One evening, Michael came home and was surprised by the fact that he felt nothing but a warm sense of well-being despite the house being messy and unkempt. Without further ado, he set out to clean up the home, trusting in his state of well-being to help him complete the task before the family came home.

"I cannot imagine why I got so irritated and frustrated by such simple matters?" wondered Michael, as he whizzed through his housekeeping chores. "I must have been a real ogre to my poor daughters."

Suddenly it dawned on him. "My goodness — I thought I was holding on to the value of Discipline — but was that really discipline?"

Broom left forgotten on the floor, Michael sank down in the nearest chair. "Discipline isn't just about setting rules and enforcing rules. True discipline is merely a means — a behavioral process — to anchor oneself to things that create a positive space of well-being," words rang loud and clear within his mind. "If it's about anchoring a sense of well-being — what on earth was I doing nagging my daughters to do something that does not resonate with their well-being or space? That doesn't make sense!"

Michael realized that he had even approached parenting in a completely unreasonable manner — justifying his attitudes to his family and home in rather terrible displays of anger and frustration. "If they discover the essence of loving the home, cleaning the home becomes second nature, not something that must be forced upon them. How simple that is!"

That evening, Michael spent some time getting feedback from his daughters on how they liked their home, and what they would do to make the home more loveable and enjoyable. Michael realized that there was a distinctive lack of relationship between his daughters and the home he thought he was so proud of. That night, he resolved to allow his family members a greater share of voice in the home — a start at least in the right direction. That night before he went to bed, Michael remembered Ian's story about Discipline.

"Do you know what my understanding of discipline was?" asked Ian during the telephone conversation. "My parents never let me call them Mum or Dad. To instill "discipline" and build "character" I had to refer to them as "Sir" and "Madam.""

"My goodness — that would have killed whatever type of affection and love between you and them!" Michael was aghast at this.

"It did — and it wasn't many, many years later, that I managed to untangle the many, many limiting beliefs I had about love, family — even the thought of having children. You see, I had what many would deem to be a spartan childhood. Because we were not wealthy, I didn't have many of the things other kids had — but whatever money my dad could spare, he invested in books and encyclopedias — building another line of discipline in me. In my parents' life experience, they had no benchmarks as to what constituted good parenting, hence the only thing they carried with them from their childhood were images and experiences of disciplinary action. Now if I had not realized and released these limiting thoughts on Discipline…"

Michael laughed and said. "If I were your son, I would have run away from home — it wouldn't be a home at all — but an army training camp!"

"Yes it would — so think about what you define as righteous discipline — and consider what it truly means to your family. Remember, they were not brought up like you were — can you imagine how it would feel to even begin to try to understand the things you do in the name of Discipline?"

Consideration

Michael's love for drinking in the pub had always been a simmering cause of complaint by his wife. And it was one particular evening when he came home twenty minutes late, he got the cold shoulder from his wife, and it did not take much to turn that into a full scale drama episode.

In the smoky aftermath, in the sulking privacy of his own study, Michael got to asking. "What just happened? My wife knows I have been a drinker all these years — but it still creates problems for her despite us being married for 16 years!"

Michael referred back to his *Sorting* and *Setting* board — and realized that he had tackled this issue with Ian months before — and that he was no drunkard. "I associate drinking at the pub with creating the space for me to relax and be with the guys — it was blameless companionship I was looking at."

"Wait a minute, she doesn't know that — maybe when I tell her about it she would understand," Michael enthused. "Heck, because of that exercise I did in *Sorting* and *Setting* my issue with that, I have already cut down my drinking by more than half!" Now Michael felt angry and resentful. "Hold it, hold it — let's get myself back on the more positive side of things here," he paused and practiced the process of uplifting his emotional state.

Having calmed himself down somewhat, Michael realized that while he had reduced his drinking and the amount of time he spent with his pals at the pub, his wife did not seem to notice the difference.

"I am being considerate to her already by drinking only before I come back, and limiting myself to 2 beers instead of 4 — but she's not noticing — even if the bills are significantly lower than before," Michael mused. "Hey, if I sat her down and told her about it, it might stop her from using it as an excuse to fight! I will go tell her right now!" But he stopped, his hand at the doorknob, suddenly recalling what Ian mentioned some months earlier.

"It doesn't matter how or why you came up with a habit or behaviour — because to another person, it may not resonate — nor make sense anyway," Ian pointed out. "What really matters is that when you approach an issue or a problem which requires two parties' involvement, you need to act *"Considerately with Compassion"* not be *"Considerate with Expectations,"* he continued.

"Hmmm, imagine if Ian was here with me, what would he say?" asked Michael out loud, picturing Ian sipping his tea in front of him.

"To do that, you need to first tell the truth with compassion. If it's some form of drama you need to have — this needing to socialize with your buddies at the pub, you need to let her know first. Secondly, you need to understand from her perspective why she feels so negatively each time you go for a drink? Is it purely concern for your health and well-being? Is it a negative emotion linked to a limiting belief she had regarding drinking? You need to

Sort and *Set* these reasons before moving forward with her," the imaginary Ian sitting in front of Michael responded sagely.

Michael suddenly realized that he had already provided himself with the answer through his imaginary conversation with Ian. He realized that unless he got into the root of any issue, any act of consideration on his end was compromised by his own ego's expectation of having done the right thing. Unfortunately, Michael knew that if compromise was in the equation no one would be truly happy.

"I guess it's time I take my wife out for a nice cup of coffee and really talk to her with compassion on this issue," sighed Michael, silently thanking his inner wisdom.

Logic — whose logic is that?

During his working hours, Michael was consistently impressed by his own level of success with his customers. At one point during a particularly fruitful week, he took some time to analyze his good fortune, hoping that he may have missed something out of his planning cycle. While busily doing his *Sorting* and *Setting* of additional goals, Michael came across a memory of his past.

"You know, business always has its ups and downs, you got to just roll with it and stay long enough to enjoy the ups again."

Those were words uttered by a Michael some years back — but words nonetheless that were formed out of belief. Michael was puzzled. Now why would his mind dredge up a statement like that? What logic would form such limiting thoughts and beliefs?

His thoughts. His beliefs.

It wasn't that long ago when he said those words, embraced those limiting beliefs. But it felt so right then — so logical.

Whose logic? That logic came from Michael. Isn't he the same Michael now? He did not specifically program his mind to act differently from before did he? His thoughts wandered back towards Ian's story of his life.

"I went through 3 cycles of debt, thanks to that thing called logic." Ian said wryly, "Earning so much money made no difference to my debts — no thanks to my twisted perception of money — and how I used it to find happiness."

"Why is that?" asked Michael.

"My ego took centre-stage, without realizing, *Sorting* or *Setting* my issues, re-*Sorting* instead to justifications and excuses especially about my own perceived generosity to people. The result? Loads of debt, and nothing to show for it. Friends I "bought" turned against me in my hour of need, resentful with the extravagant manner in which I plied my wealth on them."

Michael gaped. He never knew Ian suffered in debt before.

"But the point of the matter is — my logic took centre-stage and it was irrevocably right. Now whose logic was it?" asked Ian. "Mine. All mine. Now with *Living Kaizen*, you get to see with clarity, with your heart, how ego can manipulate logic seamlessly, subtly. Logic is merely the lies of the mind, especially when personal ego is in control."

Logic, logic, logic, words that used to mean so much to Michael, now seemingly something he could no longer trust. The more he began to *Live Kaizen*, the more in tune he was to his life purpose, and the less implications logic seemed to have on his life. Life seemed simpler, without the justifications, excuses and whys. The old Michael lived a self-fulfilling prophecy of good times and bad, of having to suffer first, and enjoying later — self inflicted logic that unfortunately attracted unequal amounts of pain and anguish — Michael shuddered at that — when all he had to do was to *Live Kaizen* — and enjoy the simplicity of life as it is, in pursuit of personal joy and happiness.

Friendliness

After one particularly amicable meeting with a headmistress, Michael sauntered out of the school feeling on top of the world. As he got into his car, Michael took a moment to recollect his conversation. How different it was now than it was before! Michael realized that apart from his improved dressing and positive demeanor, it was his friendly manner that broke the ice, breaking the headmistress out of her defensive mood. In short, he did not behave like a salesman one bit. "I was equally as polite to her as I had before, but somehow, she connected with me — why? Rifling through his notebook, Michael came across his fourth human value — Friendliness and tapped his finger absently on the word. He practiced Friendliness everywhere — but why was it becoming so different that people began to respond positively? He picked up the phone and dialed Ian's number.

"Hey, what's up?" Ian's hearty voice boomed over the cellular phone static.

Michael jumped straight to the point. "You have seen me talk to my business contacts right? I have always been friendly right? So how come I am friendly now, saying the same things, and getting outrageous results?"

"Let me put it to you in another way, remember the first time we met? When you decided to take the risk and meet up with me on a regular basis? Was I friendly?" quizzed Ian.

"Hmmm, as I recalled you were quite friendly, there was something about you that made me feel that I could spend more time with you, if not trust you then," remembered Michael.

"Yes, yes, I was really friendly. But it wasn't about what I said was it? Think about it, what was the thing that really resonated with you?" Ian pushed.

"Aaaaahhh….hang on, I felt good hearing you talk, you were so — attentive — as if whatever plans I shared were the most important thing in the world. You listened as if it mattered to you, as much as it mattered to me."

"Uh-huh. Now think about what you are doing now when you are being "friendly" to your potential customers. Think about how you feel talking to them now that you are *Living Kaizen*?" pressed Ian.

"Now every time I walk in, I have this fire within me — this really positive and exciting feeling that I am given the opportunity to share my life purpose, my work and my story with the person I am about to meet. I feel completely comfortable talking about it because it's my life's work, my passion," said Michael.

"And that is why your friendliness is so different. Friendliness is being rude politely when you aren't sincere," Ian laughed.

"That's no different than being nasty! In fact, at least when you are nasty, you are sincere in your anger. The worse thing that can happen to you is when you pretend to be nice, and the other person sees right through you. It becomes insulting to them. They feel cheated, as if you aren't treating them like a human being. That's no respect being nice when you don't feel genuinely pleased and grateful to talk to them — " suddenly Ian's line got cut off.

Michael didn't try to call back, for he already had his answer. When he reviewed his day, he realized that the 4 key values that he had discovered suddenly had far greater meaning and relevance to his life and his happiness than he thought possible.

"It's as if suddenly these words have become my guiding voice — a voice rich with compassion and love," whispered Michael softly as he gazed upon those words in his notebook. "I no longer can see things merely at face value. For me, *Living Kaizen* has given life to all that I see, and experience. There's so much I can still discover, in my journey towards fulfilling my life purpose, my life's happiness."

Michael went to bed and slept like a baby, more content and happier than he had ever been.

 Points to ponder

Employing Living Kaizen to find his core values did not give Michael the edge he thought he needed to be on the right track. It gave him cause to ponder upon the ramifications of what those values were. As he manifested Living Kaizen, Michael's experience started to reveal just how significant those values were.

Discipline was no longer a process that had to be obeyed. It became a behavioral action that allowed a person to stay grounded to things that create relevance and happiness. Michael realized that his parenting techniques weren't so much as flawed as it was misguided in its intent. He discovered that for his family to function as a family, he needed to find out what made his wife and daughters truly happy within the context of their own experience, not just his.

The value of Consideration towards another was flawed because it had expectations weighing it down. Michael discovered this to his chagrin, when his drinking trips became a cause for a nasty fight with his wife. It wasn't until he calmed himself down using Living Kaizen, that he realized that Consideration was no better than a compromise if the core belief or emotions weren't addressed using Living Kaizen's Sorting and Setting process.

Logic, once a cornerstone of Michael's belief (and ego) became dislodged as he reviewed aspects of his life for improvement. He discovered that it wasn't that long ago those thoughts grounded in scarcity seemed so comforting and safe. The means did not justify the ends, and Michael found out that he had been twisting logic rather than coming to terms with his problems back then. It was no longer safe to trust in Logic, especially when Ego was behind those thoughts. Hence, for Logic to be of value, it had to be tempered with what he felt — using his emotional guidance and not ego. This will lead to clarity of purpose.

Friendliness without sincerity is merely being rude politely, and Michael's memory was tested when he couldn't decipher the secret behind his success in meeting new clients. Michael realized that what had changed him were his beliefs, and his passion in his beliefs that led to his amazing meetings with clients.

It was indeed with great humility that Michael reviewed his core values, values that his inner wisdom had revealed to him, and unearthed a depth of compassion and humanity that was important in making his life more fulfilling and joyful.

"The irony of Life is that you can never learn enough, win enough, or succeed enough -- but the question is this -- have you savoured your time here on earth fully enough?" — *Iihann*

Chapter 8 — The big picture

Months passed.

Michael's growing business became almost routine. Michael's days were packed with purpose and meaningful experiences. *Living Kaizen* became his way of life, and as Michael focused on attaining and fulfilling his life purpose, his world manifested accordingly.

During those months, Michael began to question everything in and around his experience. No longer was he content with having opinions or laying judgments on people and events. Instead he began to ask questions, choosing to clarify and reach greater understanding.

As his life experiences manifested positively, he began to habituate *Living Kaizen*, often automatically recognizing events as mirrors to his manifested thoughts, *Sorting, Setting* and *Shining*, always with the purpose of finding greater satisfaction and joy. Practicing *Sustaining* allowed him to stay in a constant state of gratitude and joy. Embracing his *Self-Values* became the anchor point in his goal during every waking moment.

On an unconscious level, Michael was *Living Kaizen*. On a conscious level, he knew that he was happier than he had ever been. The world as he saw it began to change. Michael's daily habit of energizing his day made him step out of his home with great joy and gratitude. While he chose to fill his days with value and purpose and joy, he began to look at people around him with greater interest, often wondering if they could find their purpose and joy if they practiced *Living Kaizen*.

Michael brought this up during a rare meeting with Ian. The monsoon season was in full swing and a storm was raging outside as the evening found the two of them having a cup of coffee.

"The world suddenly seems to be a far different place for me nowadays," Michael declared.

"And so it should be — for your experience is the proof of how you are practicing *Living Kaizen*," Ian grinned.

"As I go about my days, I find myself never short of asking questions. The who, where, why, what, when and how questions often cross my mind where in the past, a logical judgment or opinion would have sufficed. No longer do I accept things as face value, but rather often ponder on the pattern or dynamics of events and of people," Michael added with wonder.

"So now you are beginning to realize that a bigger picture awaits you, only if you want to see," Ian said.

"I have spent many months re-discovering myself. At the same time, as I look within for answers, the world around me often astounds me with amazing results, yet leave me ever so hungry for greater understanding," Michael replied.

"Even my neighbours become far more complex and interesting people to me. I find that as I grow in *Living Kaizen*, the people I attract become far more 3-dimensional and interesting. I begin to wonder how I can help them, or excite them to see more than who, where, when, why, what and how they have come to be," Michael mused.

"The power we have in ourselves is far greater than we are led to believe. Once we make that life-transforming decision to take responsibility, we set into motion the first steps in *Living Kaizen*, and in change," replied Ian.

They sat in companionable silence for a moment, as raindrops clattered loudly against the windowpanes.

"How can I share this with the world? I feel that my life purpose is to give people the tool they need to make change happen," Michael asked quietly.

"You are already changing the world in your life experience. The challenge is how can you help others decide to take a chance and bring *Living Kaizen* into their life experience too," Ian leaned closer. "The people you attract will give you an indication as to how you should share this powerful life tool. Everyone needs a compass in his/her life; they just need to be in that state of mind to want it. When they do, you will be there for them."

"I am also beginning to realize that there's always a fundamental belief behind everybody's attitude and behaviour in life. What really gets me wondering is the amount of never-ending curiosity I have in wanting to know," Michael explained, pouring himself another cup.

"So now you know that everything has rhyme and reason — it's just how deep we choose to understand their beliefs, attitudes and behaviour patterns — and that serves us as a mirror in our quest for inner happiness and joy," Ian smiled.

"Isn't it amazing? Where we used to think of people as weird, or rude or nasty or crazy, we now understand that every facet of their behaviour is driven by attitudes — which must come from a set of beliefs. I am so fascinated and interested to know — even my family's behaviour consumes my interest when I am at home," Michael enthused.

"And when you reflect on how they affect or don't affect your state of mind, isn't it powerful to know that no one is responsible for your happiness but yourself?" Ian pressed.

"Absolutely!" Michael agreed. "Yet as my business takes on greater and bigger opportunities, I often ask myself this question."

"In my training, how does practicing *Living Kaizen* create excellence in the field of work? How can *Living Kaizen* apply to a thousand employees in a factory? I have experienced *Living Kaizen*, lived it and seen it reflected and manifested in my personal experience — but how can I convince a thousand, two thousand people, or school children?"

"The beauty of *Living Kaizen* is that its strength in a process — or a system that appeals to the logical minds of most people," explained Ian "When you train a thousand people, the key point you need to stress is that no matter what they do in their daily lives, taking responsibility for their actions must be the most important decision in their lives. When you share *Living Kaizen* processes with them, get them to commit to fulfilling the processes with full participation. In due course, as was with you, practicing *Living Kaizen* will open their hearts and minds."

"So the first belief I need them to commit to is to take responsibility for their own lives," said Michael.

"Yes — and wouldn't that be a powerful way to wake up a thousand minds?" Ian laughed.

"Core beliefs aren't that many, for if happiness and joy is the end result, many beliefs become very simplified and pure. When those beliefs are recognized, positive attitudes are formed automatically — and that leads to behaviour and practices that inherently raise standards and voila! Before you know it, excellence becomes continuous and a habitual way of life!" Ian snapped his fingers.

Michael smiled. "Now, every time I meet someone, I share my life purpose and story and I cannot wait to discover what the other person's beliefs, attitudes and behavioral patterns are. I am excited to find out more about myself, through communicating and sharing my passion with others."

"Once you realize that the world is a creation of people's individual beliefs, attitudes and behaviour, you will no longer judge, or be a person of prejudice. You will begin to manifest hope and positive energy, not because you can, but because it makes you feel good doing so, and when your passion and joy overflows, you can hold it in your hands and release it to the world, and watch as it manifests." Ian said.

"To master *Living Kaizen*, is to master the art of attaining joy and happiness, and excel in the life you deserve."

"It is indeed a beautiful night." said Michael, savoring the cool night breeze, as the rain faded.

"It is indeed a beautiful life. Isn't it time we find joy in it?" Ian said quietly.

Epilogue

As the final words fall from the pen, our fondest thoughts linger on the power, writing this book has unleashed. This book was written with great compassion and joy, and as such we end this amazing trip with gratitude in our hearts and hope that this book becomes a powerful compass in helping people chart their own journey to joy and happiness.

The beauty of *Living Kaizen* is that once habituated, there's no going back. As human beings, we are meant to live out our life experiences in pursuit of joy and happiness. And like the sweet things in life, once we begin to take responsibility for creating that sweetness, nothing's going to make us stop! The unlimited possibilities of using *Living Kaizen* to enjoy life are too many to be contained in this book. There will be many more adventures and experiences with *Living Kaizen*. For those who took a chance reading this, we believe that you will prosper and excel in the pursuit of happiness and hope you will join us on other *Living Kaizen* adventures.

Remember, you attracted this book to your reading experience. You have taken the first step by taking responsibility for finding your purpose. Enjoy the trip for it will truly be the most amazing adventure in your life experience.

Ganbatte!
Michael Lim and Chee Iihann

About the authors

Michael Lim

Michael prefers to call himself still a student of *Living Kaizen*, constantly discovering himself in new and wonderful ways. A trainer and consultant with more than 15 years' experience, Michael spends his time sharing and teaching his passion — *Living Kaizen*. He lives in Kuala Lumpur with his wife, 2 daughters and a dog named Coco.

Chee Iihann

After being a veteran in the communication and advertising industry for 15 years, Iihann had an epiphany — and discovered his true life's purpose. Iihann describes his life as a "fantastic adventure that's getting better and better!" Iihann devotes his time as a certified NLP (Neuro-Linguistic Programming) Coach dedicated towards helping people discover their life-purpose. He lives in Kuala Lumpur with his wife.

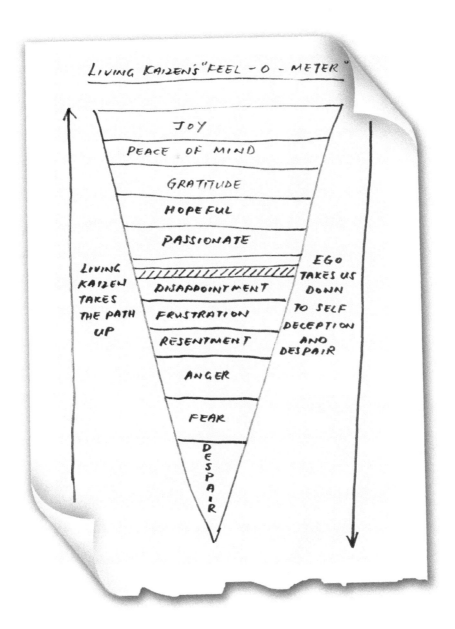

BUY A SHARE OF THE FUTURE IN YOUR COMMUNITY

These certificates make great holiday, graduation and birthday gifts that can be personalized with the recipient's name. The cost of one S.H.A.R.E. or one square foot is $54.17. The personalized certificate is suitable for framing and will state the number of shares purchased and the amount of each share, as well as the recipient's name. The home that you participate in "building" will last for many years and will continue to grow in value.

Here is a sample SHARE certificate:

HABITAT FOR HUMANITY

THIS CERTIFIES THAT
YOUR NAME HERE
HAS INVESTED IN A HOME FOR A DESERVING FAMILY

1985-2005
TWENTY YEARS OF BUILDING FUTURES IN OUR
COMMUNITY ONE HOME AT A TIME

1200 SQUARE FOOT HOUSE @ $65,000 = $54.17 PER SQUARE FOOT
This certificate represents a tax deductible donation. It has no cash value.

YES, I WOULD LIKE TO HELP!

I support the work that Habitat for Humanity does and I want to be part of the excitement! As a donor, I will receive periodic updates on your construction activities but, more importantly, I know my gift will help a family in our community realize the dream of homeownership. **I would like to SHARE in your efforts against substandard housing in my community!** *(Please print below)*

PLEASE SEND ME _____ SHARES at $54.17 EACH = $ $_____

In Honor Of: _____

Occasion: (Circle One)   HOLIDAY   BIRTHDAY   ANNIVERSARY

OTHER: _____

Address of Recipient: _____

Gift From: _____ *Donor Address:* _____

Donor Email: _____

I AM ENCLOSING A CHECK FOR $ $_____ PAYABLE TO HABITAT FOR HUMANITY <u>OR</u> PLEASE CHARGE MY VISA OR MASTERCARD *(CIRCLE ONE)*

Card Number _____ Expiration Date: _____

Name as it appears on Credit Card _____ Charge Amount $ _____

Signature _____

Billing Address _____

Telephone # Day _____ Eve _____

PLEASE NOTE: Your contribution is tax-deductible to the fullest extent allowed by law.
Habitat for Humanity • P.O. Box 1443 • Newport News, VA 23601 • 757-596-5553
www.HelpHabitatforHumanity.org

CPSIA information can be obtained
at www.ICGtesting.com
Printed in the USA
BVHW082109040719
552613BV00002B/292/P